PUBS OF
CHESHAM
and Villages

RAY EAST · KEITH FLETCHER · PETER HAWKES

To David.
Best wishes
Keith Fletcher

INTRODUCTORY NOTES

This book serves as a record of the public houses and breweries of Chesham and the surrounding Buckinghamshire villages, past and present. It is based on the photographic archive compiled by Chesham resident Ray East. It includes notes on those pubs still serving at the time of publication. The publisher welcomes correspondence regarding the photographic and textual content of this book, including errors, omissions or additions to be included in future editions.

- The front cover image is of The Sun Inn, Church Street, Chesham in 1888, photographed by William Butts

- The inside front cover image is of Church Street, Chesham, including The Golden Ball, The Seven Stars and The Two Brewers, painted by Maurice Stratford

- The title page line drawing is of The King's Arms, King Street, Chesham, drawn by Ron Quirk

- The back cover painting is of The Blue Ball, Blucher Street, Chesham, by Miss Thomasett

The Market Square, drawn by Madeleine Fletcher, was the area with the greatest density of pubs. In the listings, which are given in two alphabetical sections for the town pubs and village locations, only the historic breweries are listed, based mainly on photographic evidence. Where a date of origin is given, this may be in relation to the construction of the building, rather than the opening of the public house. Ale and beer may well have been served before the date of licensing. In the case of alternative names for pubs, the most recent name is normally given first.

First published in 2006 as a Limited Edition of 1,000 copies by Hawkes Design & Publishing

Copyright © 2006 Hawkes Design & Publishing
www.hawkesdesign.co.uk

Ray East, Keith Fletcher and Peter Hawkes have asserted their moral rights to be identified as the authors of this work.

10 digit ISBN: 0-9554707-0-6   13 digit ISBN: 978-0-9554707-0-7

A BRIEF HISTORY OF PUBS

Although the inhabitants of the British Isles have been drinking a beer-like liquor since the Bronze Age, it was not until the Romans came that the first **tabernae** (taverns) began to appear. These small huts, scattered along the new road system, were stocked to refresh the weary traveller. When the Romans departed, this feature died out, as did many other customs that they had introduced.

It was not until the Middle Ages that monasteries created guest houses and lodges to provide accommodation for travellers – usually priests and pilgrims – where bread and ale were frequently offered free of charge. Gradually some differentiation of types of establishment occurred according to what services they were legally allowed to provide. **Inns** provided rooms for travellers, **taverns** provided food and drink and **alehouses** simply served ale or beer.

Ale was originally based solely on fermented barley malt. Insanitary living conditions meant that drinking water was often dirty and unsafe, so much of the population preferred to drink **small ale,** a weak brew. The practice of including hops in the brewing process was introduced in the early 15th century, creating a new drink known as **beer**.

The origin of pub signs also goes back to the Romans, when vine leaves would be hung outside the taberna to show it sold wine. In Saxon Britain, the alewife would put an evergreen bush on a pole to let people know her brew was ready. The naming of pubs became common by the 12th century. In 1393, King Richard II decreed that, in order to identify them to the official ale taster, all pubs had to have a sign. Since most of the population was illiterate, this often took the form of a simplistic sign with religious symbols such as the The Sun, The Star or The Bell. Later they became influenced by royalty or the coat-of-arms of the landowner on whose site the pub stood.

By 1625 there were over thirteen thousand inns, taverns and ale houses in the country for a population of just five million – one for every 385 persons. With the gradual spread of the road network came the development of coaching inns, with archways leading to stable yards at the rear. Prosperous inns added private rooms where business could be discussed away from the bustling Market Square.

Comprehensive records of local pubs in the 17th century do not exist but for long periods in the 18th and 19th centuries, Chesham was able to boast a pub for every 100 persons. However, many of the pubs were comparatively small and served no more than two barrels and two dozen bottles of beer per week. Often the landlord did not rely entirely on his pub for income and carried out another occupation alongside. Today, commercial breweries have taken over many of the larger pubs whilst the smaller ones have fallen by the wayside. Those that have survived generally have a long history, in many cases as long as church establishments.

The Stag's low-ceilinged tap room with inglenook fireplace

Drinkers outside The Pheasant, in Waterside

The Breweries

Before the 19th century and the establishment of Chesham's commercial breweries, there were scores of public houses and beer shops in the town whose landlords brewed their own distinctive beer. They sold beer, stout and porter (no lager in those days), much of it made here in Chesham.

How's Brewery in Church Street was established at 80–82 Church Street in the early 19th century by Sarah How & Son. Water was obtained from a well within the property. The beer had a strong flavour attributed to the hardness of the water. Beer was stored in wooden barrels of $4\frac{1}{2}$, 9, 18 and 36 gallons. It was not kept under pressure and, in summer, open barrels were wrapped in damp cloth in an attempt to keep the beer in good condition. The brewery closed around 1900.

Barley for malting was sprouted and prepared at the malt house, previously **Darvell's Steam Brewery,** in Tap Yard off the High Street.

By far the largest of the Chesham breweries was **T & J Nash's Brewery,** situated at the foot of White Hill (originally known as Hempstead Road). Many

have recalled how the aroma of hops and barley drifted up the hill, over the railway sidings to the Whitehill School. A deep well supplied the spring water which gave a distinctive taste to the beer.

It was sold in pint, half pint and quart bottles. The brewery owned eleven Chesham pubs in 1872. It was incorporated as **The Chesham Brewery Ltd** in 1895 and took over How's Brewery in 1899.

Chesham Brewery merged with Hopcraft & Norris Ltd of Brackley in the 1930s to become **Chesham & Brackley Breweries Ltd**. Many varieties, from Pale Ale to Stout, were brewed. The brewery closed in 1957 and was demolished in 1961.

In addition to Chesham's traditional breweries, **Ellen Wallington & Son** sold non-alcoholic, home-brewed ginger beer, mineral waters and 'pop' in Victorian times. 'Codd' lemonade bottles with marble stoppers from Wallington's are still occasionally unearthed around the town.

Other local breweries serving Chesham in the past were ABC of Aylesbury, Benskin's of Watford, Bingham Cox of St Albans, Salter's of Rickmansworth, Welch's of Princes Risborough, Wheeler's of Wycombe and Weller's of Amersham.

Chesham's Town Pubs

Chesham has long been known as the town of 'boots, brushes, baptists and beer', with Cheshamites having a reputation for being hardworking, independent types, if on occasions 'a little bloody minded'. Maybe this was born of banter and argument in the drinking houses after long days of hard work in field or factory. Many of the pubs opened from 6am until 11pm, and were frequented only by working men. The furnishings were often basic, with sawdust on a bare wooden floor, and wooden settles or forms.

By 1937, around the time of the photograph above, there were 53 pubs, beer houses and off-licences serving the Chesham population of 14,000. The scene above shows lower High Street looking south. On the right can be seen **The Stag**, further along is the overhanging sign for **The George**, and the white, three storey building on the left is **The Tap**. Just out of view and opposite the Market Hall is **The Crown**.

Below are listed the Chesham pubs for which a definitive reference has been found, but for which the exact location is unknown. These are not necessarily all additional pubs – it was common for a pub to change its sign.

The Anvil And Hammer	The Cricketer's Inn, High Street	*and The Star and Garter)*
The Artichoke	The Cross Keys	The Orange Tree, Church Street
The Ball	The Good Woman	The Rising Sun
The Bear	The Jack of Newbury	The Sheaf
The Brick and Tile	The Marlborough Head	The Shears
The Castle	The Old Swan, Church Street	The Vine, High Street
The Cherry Tree, Church Street	*(between The Golden Ball*	

No.1 The Angel Inn

Location: **Francis Yard.** Dates from: **1692.** This 17th century building, now lovingly restored as an art gallery and café, is likely to have been the original inn, as 19th century documents refer to nearby buildings as 'adjoining the Angel Inn'. In 1729, the inn was described as having a gatehouse, and later as 'the best accustomed inn' in Chesham. New fronted and sashed 1753.

No.2 The Bell

Location: **109 Church Street.** Also known as: **The One Bell / The Old Bell / The Bell Beershop.** Dates from: **before 1695.** Known brewery suppliers: **Benskin's.** First licensed 1830. Legend says that the original building was a gate house for Frog Meadows (Pednor) or a tollhouse for the Missenden Road. The original building is said to have faced Pednormead rather than Church Street. Rebuilt at the turn of the century, as shown in the second photograph, which was taken at the time of the 1917 cloudburst and flood.

When it became a private residence in the early 1990s, some of the old decorative glass was retained.

No.3 The Black Horse

STILL SERVING

Location: **The Vale.** Dates from: **18th century.** Known brewery suppliers: **Wellers**. An old coaching inn, first licensed before 1822, extensively enlarged in recent times. Characterful, low-beamed interior and large country garden backing on to 'the mountain' – the hillside separating The Vale from Hawridge.

Is reputed to be haunted – reproduced below is an artist's impression of the resident ghost.

No.4 The Black Horse

Location: **Waterside,** at the foot of what is now Chessmount Rise. Also known as: **The Packhorse.** Known brewery suppliers: **Wellers.** First licensed 1778. Advertised in Metroland guidebooks as the home to the Gresham Angling Society of London. One of the last publicans was Jimmy Walker, in whose garden the box tree grew that gave its name to Box Tree Close, while Black Horse Avenue was named after the pub.

No.5 The Blue Ball

Location: **34 Blucher Street.** Dates from: **before 1736.** Known brewery suppliers: **Weller's / Benskin's.** In the latter part of the 19th century the pub also served as a slaughter house for the nearby Co-op shop. Closed in the 1960s and demolished with most of Blucher Street to allow for the St Mary's Way bypass.

No.6 The Bull and Butcher

Location: **7 Market Square.** In this detail from a painting by Thomas Fisher, made c.1810, the pub may already have become a private house, although there seems to be the shape of an animal's head by the door. Later the building became the town's Post Office, pictured. Smith's stationers took over the building in 1894 and well over a century later, the same line of business is continued here.

No.7
The Carpenters Arms

Location: **6 Blucher Street.**
Known brewery suppliers:
**Chesham Brewery (Nash
Bros).** First licensed 1830.
Demolished in the 1960s
along with the rest of the
terrace. The plan shows its
position in relation to
The Star public house.

No.8 The Chequers Inn

Location: **12 Market Square.** Known brewery suppliers: **Wellers.** First licensed 1756. Competed with
The Crown, offering teas and 'good accommodation for cyclists'. Now the head office of 'The Chesham',
the oldest existing Building Society in the world.

No. 9 The Cock Tavern

Location: **The Broadway**. Known brewery suppliers: **Salter's / Greenalls.**
First licensed 1736. The original building was advertised by a simple sign
depicting a cockerel. Rebuilt in the 19th century and was a backdrop to many
town centre gatherings. Has become a basic pub serving local drinkers.

No. 10
The Crown Inn

Location: **1 High Street**. Also known as: **The Crown Hotel.**
Dates from: before **1579**, when John West was 'mine holder of the
Crowne.' Known brewery suppliers: **Cannon Ales / Taylor
Walkers**. Headquarters of the Parliamentary forces in the district
during the Civil War of 1642. General Wolfe is believed to have
stopped the night on his way from London to Liverpool before
sailing for Quebec. Featured a large galleried courtyard and later
incorporated the Victoria Hall Restaurant & Lounge. Demolished
to make way for a supermarket – one of Chesham's greatest losses.

№.11 The Eagle

Location: **Waterside,** opposite the coalyard that was situated by The Pheasant. Also known as: **The Spread Eagle**. First licensed before 1822. Closed in 1900. The photograph shows The Eagle at the end of a terrace of Victorian cottages leading out to the fields. All this has been swept away by flats and houses built on the hillsides.

№.12 The Elephant and Castle

Location: **Waterside.** Known brewery suppliers: **Wheeler's.** First licensed 1830. Extensively enlarged in 1966. This part of Waterside has been substantially developed, firstly with the expansion of Marshall's car garage, now with new flats. Today's pub is regaining popularity and offers Chinese take-away food.

STILL SERVING

No. 13
The Five Bells

Location: **282 Waterside,** at the foot of Inkerman Terrace. Known brewery suppliers: **Welch's.** First licensed 1857. Closed in 1918. Stood adjacent to Joseph La Verne's New Prospect Steam Sawmills. Landlord Henry Wingrove's cellar door can be seen to the left; the entrance to the pub was accessed via the yard.

No. 14
The Foresters Tavern

Location: **98 Waterside.** Dates from: **1857.** Known brewery suppliers: **Welch's / ABC.** The Foresters Society met here. It also had a parlour, sometimes called 'the singing room', where customers would make their own entertainment in the days before television and radio. The last landlords were Mr Green and Mr Brownsell. The pub closed in 1933 and became a lodging house. Today the building has been converted to private residences.

No. 15
The Fox and Hounds

Location: **Market Square,** (the building to the far left of the photograph) which was to the right of The Chequers.

It closed in the mid-19th century and became home to The Chesham Mechanics Institute. The artist's impression shows how The Fox and Hounds may have looked before a Victorian shopfront was added.

No. 16 The Gamekeepers Lodge

STILL SERVING

Location: **Bellingdon Road.** Also known as: **The Griffin.** Known brewery suppliers: **Chesham Brewery.** First licensed 1889. It has recently undergone a major transformation, and despite its urban setting now has the feel of a country pub with a characterful interior. Features a wartime corner with associated memorabilia, and a large collection of framed photographs of Chesham's public houses.

At the rear of The Gamekeepers Lodge, in the old stable block, is Chesham Museum, established August 2004. There is a permanent display on the '4 Bs of Chesham': beer, boots, brushes and baptists. Visit the website: www.cheshammuseum.org.uk for more details and opening times.

No.17 The George and Dragon

Location: **High Street.** Also known as: **The George Inn / The George Hotel.** Known brewery suppliers: **Taylor Walkers / Ind Coope / Benskin's.** Dates from: **15th century or earlier, refronted 1715.** Became a licensed coaching inn in 1622. In the 1790s, the stage-coach would set out from The George Inn for the Bell & Crown at Holborn, a journey which took five hours. The mail coach also left from here, and in later decades there were horse buses to Berkhamsted and Watford Railway Stations.

In the early 19th century the magistrates court was held at The George. During renovation in 1971 two historic murals were found on the walls in the upper rooms. The building, with its dark and characterful interior and cobbled yard, is now scheduled for its architectural and historic interest and is a popular town centre establishment.

STILL SERVING

No. 18 The Globe

Location: **Market Square,** to the left of The Chequers. In this detail of a painting of Market Square by Thomas Fisher, from c.1810, The Globe is the double roofed building with an overhanging sign. By 1842 the pub also served as a bakehouse. Since demolition of its neighbours, the building stands on the corner of Market Square and now features signage welcoming visitors to Chesham, listing market days in the High Street as Wednesdays and Saturdays.

No. 19 The Golden Ball

Location: **Church Street.** Dates from: **17th century.** Known brewery suppliers: **Weller's / Benskin's** (1929) **/ Ind Coope.** Landlord from 1905 to 1960 was Harry Wing, famed for running a 'knackers yard' behind the pub and being a horse dealer. Home to the Customs & Excise Office for many years and host to the National Union of Farmers meetings. Closed 1985 and now serves as offices.

No.20 *The Horse and Jockey*

Location: **58 & 60 Germain Street.** Dates from: **earliest reference is 1723.** Known brewery suppliers: **Chesham Brewery (Nash Bros.)** Was originally five, then three, then two cottages and part of the Bury Manor. First licensed as a public house in 1830 when it was called **The Dolphin.** Listed as a beershop in 1842. By 1843 it had become The Horse & Jockey. It was purchased by the Nash family of Chesham Brewery for £550 in 1897. It had closed by 1914, when it was owned by William Rose, who played the piano for the silent movies at Chesham's Empire and Palace cinemas. It later served as a second-hand furniture shop run by William's wife Montague.

No.21 *The Huntsman*

Location: **103 High Street**, just beyond Collin's store on the left of the photograph. Previously known as: **The Green Man** (1842). Known brewery suppliers: **Wellers.** First licensed in 1838. The 'Penny Gaff', a travelling theatre, often performed here. Demolished to make way for the first High Street Co-op stores in 1920.

No.22 The Jolly Sportsman

Location: **Broad Street**. First licensed in 1843. Renovated and extended in 1962. Its front yard was removed with the construction of Khartoum Road, later known as Eskdale Avenue. The photograph shows a group setting out for the Ascot Races in 1903. Regulars used to be mainly local tradesmen and boot and shoe makers. Today, The Jolly Sportsman is an unpretentious pub serving local residents.

STILL SERVING

No.23 The King's Arms

Location: **Germain Street / King Street.** Also known as: **The Old King's Arms.** Dates from: **18th century,** much restored. First licensed before 1822. The pub and its location by the old town remain attractive.

STILL SERVING

No.24 The Lamb

Location: **58 High Street.** Dates from: **1840,** when it was set back from the row of shops (picture A). Rebuilt as a two storey building (picture B, right), then extended **c.1870** with a third storey and given a decorative frontage with pargeting on the top floors (picture C). Known brewery suppliers:

Nash's (Chesham Brewery) / Ind Coope. (Wallington's of Waterside delivered non-alcoholic beverages.) Also offered a livery stables, with the landlord keeping 14 horses at one time. Following alterations to the entrance and general modernisation (picture D), The Lamb developed a reputation in the 1950s and '60s as Chesham's 'den of iniquity'. Closed in 1974 and was demolished soon after, despite protests from the Chesham Society.

No.25 The Mermaid

Location: At the foot of **Trapps Lane,** opposite old China Bridge, with its entry by Christchurch. Further along, opposite Lord's Mill by 'Bass's stile', was an unnamed pub run by Theophilus Plato, the scrivener.

No.26 The Mermaid

Location: **60 Church Street.** Also known as: **The Bugle** (unconfirmed later name). First licensed 1753. The pub occupied two cottages with a yard, which are the furthest ones along the left of the street in the photograph, situated on the rise in the road known as 'The Nap', just before the entrance to The Bury. The pub also included Mr Wingrove's butchers shop at one time. It became very dilapidated and was demolished in the early 1960s to be replaced by a rather modern house.

No.27 The Misty Moon

Location: **upper High Street.** Also known as: **The Last Post** (until 2006). Dates from: **1994.** Chesham's newest pub was set up in the town's old post office building, which was originally built in 1625 – it features a magnificent chimney dating from that time. The contemporary interior is warm and welcoming, with much local historical information on the walls. It has remained deservedly popular.

No. 28 The Nag's Head

Location: **Red Lion Street.**
Dates from: **1695.** Known brewery suppliers: **Weller's / Benskin's.**
It originally contained stables, then a garage. For many years the sheep market was held in the open yard in front of the pub. The landlord from 1905 until 1937 was Frederick (Toby) Lewis, who was also a cricketer, known as 'stone wall Toby'. There was an old barn at the rear of the pub where 'bean feasts' were held – large parties used to come from London for these feasts, where the fare was boiled beef, carrots, onions and tomatoes with plum puddings as big as footballs boiled in a cloth, plus of course, beer. In the Nag's Head Meadow next door was the roller skating rink; also silent films were shown and 'Penny Grafs' were held. Travelling showmen from London would put on plays such as *Penny Martin in the Red Barn*. When it was demolished for road widening in 1937, the license was transferred to the new Red Lion.

No. 29 The Nash Arms

Location: **Vale Road.** Also known as: **The Nashleigh Arms.** Dates from: **mid-19th century.** Known brewery suppliers: **Chesham Brewery / Ind Coope.** Built to serve the growing local community in Newtown, the pub also offered weekend accommodation for visitors to the surrounding countryside. It is still frequented by local drinkers and its cavernous Victorian interior is popular for social gatherings and events.

STILL SERVING

No.30 The New Inn

Location: **237 Berkhampstead Road.** First licensed 1860. Served the residents of Alexander Street and George Street and the workers from the local boot factories and sawmills. Demolished February 1971.

No.31 The New Inn

Location: **144 Waterside.**
Also known as: **The New Engine** due to its proximity to the railway bridge. First licensed in 1869. Known brewery suppliers: **Benskin's.** The landlord for many years was Chesham's WWI hero, Alfred Alexander Burt, VC.

Mr Tuffney took over in 1950 and remained as landlord until his death in 1965, when the pub closed. It had, only one year earlier, obtained a full wine and spirits license, being the last pub in Chesham to do so. At the rear was a stable and yard, home for many years to Chesham's 'rag and bone' man. The building was demolished in 1971 and replaced with flats.

No.32 The Old Sun

Location: **Church Street**, opposite the bidwell. Also known as: **The Sun Inn / The Old Sun Lodging House.** Dates from: between **1430 and 1450** according to some reports, although others put it later in the **16th century.** Known brewery suppliers: **Bingham Cox.** Originally served as a lodging house for pilgrims visiting the church. In the upper rooms religious texts were found on the wattle and daub. Later became an inn and finally a resting place for tramps and vagrants.

Some historians claim that some time between 1636 and 1700 it was home to Roger Crabbe, Chesham's mad hatter. In Victoria's reign the establishment operated its own brewery but by 1888 was taking ales from the brewery owned by William Cox of St Albans. The fine building with its oversailing storey was taken down in 1936 and moved piece-by-piece to a field called Flecridge, at Pednor, where it still stands as a fine private house. Old coins dating back to 1730 were found under the floor of the old tap room while other discoveries included a baby's shoe of a similar age, a lace bobbin and a knife. The last landlord was Daniel Frenc, who was licensed to sell beer, porter, perry, cider and tobacco.

No.33 The Pheasant

Location: **Waterside.** Dates from: **1860.** Known brewery suppliers: **Benskin's.** Extensively re-modelled in 1963 with the addition of

STILL SERVING

an extension, an off-licence sales area and a kitchen upstairs. Benefits from an attractive riverside garden and play area, with the result that the pub is popular with locals and visitors alike, especially in the summer months.

No.34 The Plough

Location: **1 Broad Street,** on the corner of Hempstead Road (White Hill).
Known brewery suppliers: **Chesham Brewery.** First licensed in 1830. With its location practically opposite Chesham Brewery, the beer barrels could be rolled across the road straight into the cellar. Russell's brushmakers began business here in the 1840s when

Charles Russell started selling brushes as a sideline to beer. Later, for a period of over 60 years, the pub was run by the Priest family, who also kept a haulage business at the adjoining building, starting after WWI. When this failed, the business was turned into a garage. In the 1940s the pub provided 60 to 70 lunches every week day for local factory workers. It closed in 1960, shortly after Chesham Brewery, and was demolished to make way for shops, flats and a petrol station, the latter since converted to a dry cleaners.

No.35 The Prince's Arms

Location: **Wey Lane/Missenden Road junction,** opposite The Queen's Head. Also known as: **The Prince of Wales.** Known brewery suppliers: **Chesham Brewery.** First licensed 1840. Now two private residences.

No.36 The Punch Bowl

Location: **Red Lion Street** (formerly The London Road). Also known as: **The Prince of Wales.** Dates from: **before 1758.** The Brotherly Society of Tradesmen met here. It was sold for £300 in about 1897 and demolished to make way for the Hinton Chapel (now Trinity Baptist Church).

No.37 The Queen's Head

Location: **Church Street.** Known brewery suppliers: **Weller's / Benskin's / Brakspears / Fullers.** First licensed 1746. Traditional glazed brick headers are a feature of the building. A few doors to the left is Lantern House, where beer and porter were brewed in the early 18th century. The Queen's Head is probably Chesham's most traditional and unspoilt pub, and with its location in the old town by the river, is extremely popular with locals and visitors alike. Extended in the 1990s to allow for a Thai restaurant, run in conjunction with the pub.

STILL SERVING

No.38 The Red Lion

Location: **Red Lion Street,** on the corner with Germain Street. Also known as: **Red Lion Inn.** Dates from: **1723,** replaced **1937.** Known brewery suppliers: **Benskin's.** Mrs Sarah Ann Ragflan was the last licence holder of the old pub (picture B), having taken it on from her father. The tables in the tap room were scrubbed white and there was a spittoon in the corner. Until the new police station was opened in 1932 a coroner's court was held on the first floor of the pub and dead bodies were placed in the stables behind the inn, via Red Lion Yard (picture A). The Town Crier, Philip Howard, was said to have lived in one of the stables too. The landlord was licensed to let horses in 1863 and the pub was much visited by the Old Berkeley Hunt. Road widening meant demolition, and Benskin's came up with a grand scheme in the early '30s (picture C). It was several years later that work, by Jesse Mead Ltd, on a less ostentatious pub began behind the existing building (picture D), with bricks and tiles from the old pub reclaimed and used to build a house in Tylers Hill.

The '30s style pub (picture E) was reorganised in the 1990s (picture F) with a resulting major boost in trade, especially from the younger generation.

STILL SERVING

No.39 The Rose and Crown

Location: **Waterside.** Dates from: **1830.** Known brewery suppliers: **Fuller's.** Kept at one time by the Wallington family. Ellen Wallington & Son made the local aerated waters and cordials that were popular in Victorian times. This photograph from 1868 shows the millpond of Lord's Mill on the left, with the Waterside road leading to the substantial, gabled frontage of the pub.

Many of the older properties on the riverside were occupied by duck breeders, with the large, white Aylesbury duck being a favourite.

The pub sign (above), seen between the two right hand gables of the Rose & Crown, is that of the Five Bells, situated at the end of the terraced Victoria Place.

The Rose & Crown today is a community pub, with a traditional and welcoming interior..

No.40 The Royal Oak

Location: **88/90 Upper High Street.** Also known as: **The Old Royal Oak.** Dates from: **late 17th century.** The pub building (far left in the photograph) was later occupied by a toy shop, then Scamps Wine Bar. In 1988 it was destroyed by a massive gas explosion. Following demolition of the old pub, the site has remained empty and boarded up – an eyesore in the town centre.

No.41 The Seven Stars

Location: **12 Church Street.** First licensed in 1753. Its simple sign can be seen here from two opposite directions, white on one side, black on the other. The pub was kept by Jesse Barnes, who also ran a wheeler's shop here in 1842. This part of Church Street was swept aside by the St Mary's Way road scheme.

No.42 The Stag

Location: **38 High Street.** Known brewery suppliers: **ABC.** First licensed in 1853 and bought by the Aylesbury Brewery Company in 1873, it was run by the Abbott family for 60 years. From 1918 the pub was combined with a green grocery business and with its single entrance became known as the 'secret drinkers' pub'. There was a cellar at the back and stables at the rear. As there was no other entrance the horses were led in and out through the front door, as illustrated. Mr Abbott's favourite trick was to nail a florin to the floor and then watch the antics of the drinkers trying to pick it up. Demolished in 1937.

No.43 The Star Inn

Location: **2 Blucher Street.** Known brewery suppliers: **Salter's.** First licensed before 1822. 17th century building with a carved oak bargeboard under the gable, a relic of the wood carver's art. The photograph below, showing The Star's simplistic sign, is one of the earliest images of Chesham, dating from the mid-19th century. Just out of view is the old Baptist chapel, replaced in 1902 with the magnificent Broadway Baptist Church.

The Star served as a TB clinic before it was demolished around the beginning of WWII, along with the eight small dwellings in Star Yard, to make way for the town's first major car park.

No.44 The Star and Garter

Location: **57 Church Street.** Known brewery suppliers: **Chesham Brewery / Wellers.** First licensed 1832. Described as Chesham's last 'spit and sawdust' pub, it closed in 1936 and was altered to become an antiques shop. At this time a wooden notice board was found, bearing the date 27th August 1838. It gave the licensing hours as follows: 'Hour of opening between the 10th of October and the 6th day of April – six o'clock in the morning. Hour of closing between those periods –

nine o'clock in the evening. Hour of opening between the 6th day of April and the 10th day of October – five o'clock in the morning. Hour of closing between those periods – ten o'clock in the evening'.

No.45 The Tap

Location: **27 High Street.** Known brewery suppliers: **Chesham Brewery.** First licensed 1853. At the rear it had a malt house and brewery (at one time known as Darvell's Steam Brewery), which closed at the end of the 19th century. In the late 1940s the Chesham Town Prize Silver Band used to practice at The Tap; about this time the pub was completely rebuilt in mock tudor style

(see inset), but can have lasted only a relatively short time, as it closed in January 1960, to be demolished once again and replaced by a retail unit.

No.46 The Three Tuns

Location: **White Hill.** Dates from: **1750,** originally a blacksmith's shop. Rebuilt in **1895.** Closed in 1964 but was taken over as offices by the Chesham Council Surveyors' Department. Demolished in 1976.

By the sharp bend of White Hill (which caused the problem the authorities cited for the demolition of The Three Tuns, on road safety grounds), there is now a broad grassy verge and a rough hewn stone which serves as a memorial to the martyr Thomas Harding who was burnt at the stake in a dell just above this spot.

No.47
The Two Brewers

Location: **Church Street.** The Tithe Map of 1842
shows this pub five doors up from The Seven Stars,
and owned by Thomas Fassnidge, junior. It also
comprised of a woodhouse and yard, the entrance
to which can be seen on the left hand side of Church
Street in the photograph, with the sign above.
Practically all of the buildings in the mid-ground were
demolished with the construction of St Mary's Way,
with the exception of The Golden Ball, far right.

No.48 The Unicorn

Location: **Bois Moor Road.** Dates from: **1889.** Also known as: **The Unicorn Hotel**; was to have been
called **The Railway Hotel** because the original plans were to terminate the railway on The Moor behind
the pub. Was half in Chesham and half in Chesham Bois, with different licensing hours in each side of the
pub. In July 1944 Robert Arbib, an American soldier, told the *Bucks Examiner* 'I shall not forget the friendly
evenings at The Unicorn, where we buy each other rounds of ale and argue through the haze, and settle all
the problems that baffle the world'. It closed in the late 1990s and became a children's play school.

No.49 The Waggon and Horses

Location: **152 High Street.** Dates from: **mid 18th century** but rebuilt in about **1900.** Known brewery suppliers: **Salter's /Ind Coope.** In the large photograph below, immediately behind the horse, was a forge from where it is reputed that burning embers were taken to light the pyre on which 16th century martyr Thomas Harding was burnt. The sign on the wall advertises Winkley & Shaw, Horse Slaughteres, and also Climpson & Son. Joseph Climpson (pictured with his family) held the licence here for fifty years and began a long association of the Climpsons with the licensed trade in Chesham. He also ran a carriers business; mail was left at the pub and farmers from the outlying areas would call to collect it. Another sideline was the carrying of hay and straw, and his son Ernest drove the wagon to London three times a week. When Joseph died in 1890 his wife Sophia took over the license until her death in 1899. Ernest later opened a wine and spirits shop in Blucher Street and the family continued to trade there until 1976. Had a large garden at the rear with stables, until lost to the northern end of St Mary's Way. Today's recently painted frontage shows off this town centre pub to good effect.

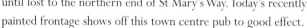

STILL SERVING

No.50 *The Wild Rover*

Location: **Amersham Road** by The Pound.
Known brewery suppliers: **Ind Coope.**
Also known as: **The Waggoner's Rest /
The White Horse.** First licensed 1838.
In the photograph, Mr Whittle stands with his
family in the forecourt of the White Horse.
Today's renamed and much extended pub is
frequented by those who live and work locally.

STILL SERVING

No.51 *The White Lion*

Location: **26 Red Lion Street**. First licensed in 1844, this pub is not to be confused with the better
known White Lion which once stood in Townfield Yard. The last landlord was Frederick Turner. The building
can be seen on the far right in the old photograph, beyond Hyatt's Yard and the original Zion Chapel.

No.52
The White Lion

Location: **Townfield Yard.** Known brewery suppliers: **Welch's / ABC.** First licensed in 1868. One time landlord was John Hayes, who started a shoe making business here and later had a shoe factory built in Waterside which was carried on by his son John. A place where 'knights of the road' could sleep for a shilling a night. Townfield Yard was squalid and insanitary, notorious for being a rough area and a trouble spot. The pub, along with the complete terrace, was demolished in 1937. However, if the Yard had been saved, it would most likely now be a picturesque and valuable row of cottages.

THE BEER SHOPS

Beer shops were very numerous throughout the town in times past. There were, in fact, too many to list here with any purpose. As an example of their proliferation, listed below are those beer shops which operated in Chesham in 1889:

Waterside – Nos. 95, 144, 185, 272 and 422
Red Lion Street – No. 30
Townfield Yard – No. 41
Germain Street – No. 10
Church Street – Nos. 10 and 82
High Street – No. 52
Station Road – No. 30
Townsend Road – No. 35

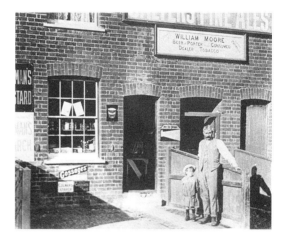

Illustrated are two fondly remembered beer shops: William Moore's of Townsend Road, advertising Salter's Fine Ales. William's son Archie, pictured as a boy, later took over the business. Below is Nellie Giles' beer shop in Alexander Street, opened in 1897. Nellie opened from 8am to 10pm six days a week and for five hours on a Sunday. The shop was demolished in 1971 following a compulsory purchase for new flats.

Village Pubs Around Chesham

The Buckinghamshire villages surrounding Chesham are sited on the ridges and hilltops of the Chilterns, often on common land, greens and heaths originally cleared for agriculture and settlement. The word **'leah'**, means 'clearing' and from it are derived the names of Ashley Green, Botley, The Lee, Ley Hill, Lye Green and Whelpley Hill.

As with the town, the villages were well catered for by public houses. Originally the drinking establishments served not only the local community, but also cattle drovers and travellers. Gradually people from the town began visiting the villages to drink, in particular young men whose parents had enrolled them, as children, into the various Temperance Societies, and who could go out to drink in the villages anonymously. Frequently, the pubs became the centre of village life.

Pictured: **The Swan** and **The Crown** by Ley Hill common; regulars of **The Plough** at Hyde Heath, with landlord Frank Morton; and visitors to **The Bull** at Bellingdon.

ASHERIDGE

No. 1 The Blue Ball

Dates from: **18th century**. Also known as:
The Asheridge Arms.

Known brewery suppliers: **Weller's.** The photographer's family
and horse & trap also appear in the photo of The Bull at Bellingdon.
Closed temporarily, but set to continue as a vital part of village life.

ASHLEY GREEN

No. 2 The Golden Eagle

Dates from: **1856**. Also known as: **The Eagle.** Known brewery suppliers: **Chesham Brewery.** Situated next to
the site of the village smithy, which survived until the mid-20th century. Like many pubs, there are claims that it
is haunted. The landlady at one time was the sister of Phyllis Culvert, the film actress. Now a Grade II listed
building, the pub is at the centre of a thriving community. It still offers a characterful and traditional venue for
the enjoyment of good food and drink.

BALLINGER

No.3 The Pheasant

First licensed in the mid-nineteenth century. It was sold in 1906 to the Haddock family for £75. The Pheasant has recently come under new management and comprises The Hatters Restaurant & Bar. It is considered an important part of the village, but is frequented by visitors to the area as much as it is by the local community. Overlooks the village green and was once home to Ballinger Cricket Club.

No.4 The Bull

First licensed in 1822. It closed in 1974 and is now a private residence, Mortimer House.

BELLINGDON

No.5 The Bull

Dates from: **mid-18th century.** Originally two cottages, one becoming registered as a beer house in 1830 and run by Lydia Blackwell, whilst her husband Richard ran a grocers shop in the cottage next door. By 1900, when Mr Newman took it over as landlord, the pub occupied both cottages. For much of the early part of the 20th century it was home to Bellingdon Cricket Club which played in a field at the back. The property still includes 17 acres of land. From 1891 to 1900 the landlord was John Howard, who also ran a brickworks in Bellingdon. The pub was considerably altered about 20 years ago and now has a reputation for good food.

No.6 The Golden Perch

Near to the site of St Johns Church. Its early history is unknown. Was kept by Henry Barnes in 1843 and by William Franklin, a cordwainer in 1851. Closed as a public house in the late 19th century and became a private residence, Church Cottage, which was demolished in the 1960s.

BOTLEY

No.7 The Botley Rover

Dates from: **19th century.** Location: junction of **Botley Road and Botley Lane**, then just a footpath (right of photograph). A beer house, later converted into three cottages with the cellar remaining under the one at the Ley Hill end. Later replaced by a single dwelling.

No.8 The Five Bells

Dates from: **17th century**. First licensed 1857. Extended in 1976. A former owner was the world famous golfer Sandy Lyle. Closed in 2002.

No.9 The Hen & Chickens

Location: **Botley Road**, on the old trade route to Ley Hill and Bovingdon. Known brewery suppliers: **Chesham Brewery / Salter's**. First licensed before 1822. Occupies a row of c.17th century cottages which probably extended further to the right; the original timbers and nogging remain within the pub, despite alterations. The barn end was originally a livery stable and coal depot run by Mr Grace, whose wife transformed it into a bar selling beer from a scrubbed wooden table.

BUCKLAND COMMON

No.10
The Boot and Slipper

Dates from: **1698.** Also known as: **The Boot** until 1860. William Miles was the original registered innkeeper. Known brewery suppliers: **Roberts & Williams** (Ivinghoe) / **Benskin's** (1928). Closed as a licensed premises in April 1976 and is now a private residence.

CHARTRIDGE

No. 11 The Britannia

Known brewery suppliers: **Benskin's** (1931). Kept at one time by Mrs Gomm, who had bacon hanging from the ceiling and would cut off slices and fry them for customers. When the renewal of the licence was refused it finally closed as a public house on 31st December 1939. It is now a private house known as The Old Britannia.

No. 13 The Bell

First licensed 1862. Known brewery suppliers: **Weller's.** Seen on the right of the photograph above, when it was an alehouse, and The Portobello Arms, opposite, sold spirits. Now an important village pub serving the expanding community, and offering good food and a traditional pub atmosphere.

No. 12 The Horse and Hounds

STILL SERVING

No. 14 The Portobello Arms

First licensed before 1822. In 1839 it was run by Hannah Dwight who also offered groceries and bread. Now a residential property.

Earliest reference to a beerhouse is 1863 when it was **The Rose and Crown**. Known brewery suppliers: **Chesham Brewery**. The earliest deed of this property was dated 1814 when the owner was Thomas Amsden, a straw plait dealer of Tring. Closed for substantial modernisation in 1967 when it was re-opened and renamed. Was damaged by fire in 1990 and has now been restored as a private house.

CHOLESBURY

No. 15 *The Blue Ball*

Exact location uncertain. Dates from: **mid-18th century**. Later became **The Nine Pin Bowl** but was shortlived.

No. 16 *The Castle*

Exact location uncertain. Dates from: **mid-18th century.** Was short lived. Kept by Joseph Batchelor from 1753 to 1763.

No. 17
The Bricklayers Arms

Building dates back to **1606**. The pub was licensed to Anthony Carpenter in 1753 and known as **The Maidenhead.** Renamed by 1883. Until 1924 kept by James Pallett, who was also a timber and coal merchant and an undertaker, who bought the pub from the **Aylesbury Brewery Company** in 1920.

Closed in 1924 and is now called Bury House, a private residence. The inglenook fireplace has been retained by the current owners.

No. 18 *The Queens Head*

Next door to the Bricklayers Arms was a beerhouse kept in 1843/47 by Daniel Bishop and owned by William Ayres. The property has long been demolished.

No. 19 *The Slip Inn*

Nothing is known of the history of this pub. It was part demolished but some of the walls remain within the private property pictured.

CHIVERY

No. 20 *The Plough*

Dates from: **1766.** Continued until 1913 when it was supplied by **Chesham Brewery**. Later it became a restaurant, tea rooms and general store and is now a private residence.

HAWRIDGE

No.21 The Full Moon

Earliest record as an alehouse in 1693 called the **Half Moon.** Became **The Moon** in 1812 and The Full Moon in 1883. Served as the home for the Lord of The Manor's Court. Also home to the Cholesbury Bowls Club (with green) and served as clubhouse and changing rooms for Hawridge and Cholesbury Cricket Club. The name of the brewers **Wethered's** appears in the records in 1838. Major alterations in the 1990s gave more room to serve wholesome food in the ambience of a 17th century pub.

STILL SERVING

No.22 The Mermaid

Dates from: **17th century**. First became a public house in 1753 when the registered licensee was Martin Fuller. The building was re-fronted, raised and extended in the 18th century. It has a late 18th century brick and flint extension to the rear and an old tile roof parallel to the main roof. Between 1801 and 1838 the building was converted into three cottages.

No.23 The Rose & Crown

First licensed in 1749. In 1913 the brewers **Lock & Smith** of Berkhamsted sold it to **Benskin's**. A full licence was granted in December 1957. The pub is reputed to be haunted, although three ghosts have been exorcised. Today it offers great food and a friendly atmosphere in a beautiful country setting.

STILL SERVING

HYDE END

No.24 Annie Baileys

First licensed 1851. Known brewery suppliers: **Weller's.** Also known as: **The Barley Mow.** Renamed in 2002 after the landlady from the 1840s of The Red Lion in Cuddington, Bucks, which closed in 2000. The Barley Mow was transformed to become an up-market bar and restaurant with a stunning Italianate patio area.

STILL SERVING

HYDE HEATH

No.25 The Eagle

Dates from: **1860**. The neighbouring cottages are now the site of Heath Motors but the pub building (far right in the photo) remains as a private house.

No.26 The Plough

First licensed 1830. Known brewery suppliers: **Weller's / Benskin's.** The Plough, under landlord Frank Morton, had a public bar, a small saloon bar, and a small off-sales bar separating the two. It provided entertainment in the form of a piano, with darts, dominoes and draughts played in the public bar. The Plough is still a thriving and popular pub today.

No.27 The Red Cow

Known brewery suppliers: **Benskin's.** First licensed 1830. The pub was very basic, with a floor strewn with sawdust, a beer barrel on the end of a wooden table, a wooden bench for seating, and a spittoon in the corner. Mrs Franklin, mother of Charles Franklin who delivered coal by horse and cart in Hyde Heath and neighbouring villages, kept the Red Cow, part of which still stands in the yard of Redlands next to the church.

No.28 The Wheatsheaf Inn

Location: **Brown's Road.** First licensed 1830. This pub was mentioned in *An English Gamekeeper*, a book published in 1892 by John Wilkins. Wilkins was a gamekeeper on the estates of the Fuller family, who lived at Germain House, Chesham. One of the Fuller's under-keepers was sacked for 'being too fond of visiting The Red Cow, The Boot and Slipper, The Wheatsheaf and other houses of call'. He turned poacher. The illustration is from Wilkin's book.

THE IDENTIFICATION OF "COUGHTREY, THE POACHER," BY THE OLD WOMEN OF THE VILLAGE.

LATIMER

No.29 The Cavendish Arms

Dates from: **18th century.** Coaching inn kept by John Dickinson in 1851, with stabling for two horses and nearby cover for coaches. The second Lord Chesham closed it and by 1900 it was the village schoolmaster's house. In the 1930s it was converted and sold as a private house.

LEE COMMON

No.30 The Bugle

First licensed in 1845. Closed in 1951 but re-opened in 1971. Sadly, it closed again a few years ago. Was run by the Holloway family from 1845 until 1951.

No.31 Old Inn House

Also in the village is this private residence, to which no original name has been attributed, but where the sighting of a ghost has been reported.

LEE GATE

No.32 The Gate Inn

First licensed before 1822. A free-house specialising in ciders during the 1970s until a small brewery was installed in an adjacent barn by the owner Peter Carr. This produced 25 barrels per week of best or ordinary bitter. Currently a well preserved country pub, but only open at weekends.

STILL SERVING

LEY HILL

No.33 The Crown

Also known as: **The Rose and Crown**. First licensed before 1822. Known brewery suppliers: **Chesham Brewery.** The original building was destroyed by fire, but rebuilt and modernised in 1932. The pub was

home to Chesham & Ley Hill Golf Club for nearly 50 years until it transferred to its own clubhouse in 1965. The substantial dwelling between the two pubs was removed some decades ago. The Crown is now well known for its good food and live music.

STILL SERVING

No.34 The Swan

STILL SERVING

Dates from: **1520,** modified in **1680.** One of the oldest pubs in Bucks.

It consists of a timber framed building which originally formed three cottages. The Swan served as an alehouse for many centuries, and is known for its association with the requests for a 'last and final ale' from condemned prisoners on their way to the gallows by Jasons Hill. Today's pub offers a warmer welcome with fine cuisine, fine wines and real ales, which can be enjoyed in the restaurant, characterful 'snug', or large garden.

LYE GREEN

No.35 The Black Cat

Also known as: **The White Horse**. First licensed in 1838. For many years it was the centre of village life, where local families held parties and celebrations. During the 1940s and '50s the landlords were Mr and

Mrs Pratt, who allowed Bessie Bangay from St. George's Church, Tylers Hill and the District Nurse, Margaret Bly, to hold church meetings in the sitting room. It was the headquarters of Lye Green cricket team who played in a field behind the pub.

These days, home cooked food is served throughout the week. There is a large garden and play area. Villagers also have the benefit of a function room.

STILL SERVING

SOUTH HEATH

No.36 The Black Horse

Location: **Frith Hill**. Known brewery suppliers: **Benskin's.** Now the Weights & Measures Fitness Club.

No.37 The Lamb

Location: **Potter Row**. Known brewery suppliers: **Chesham Brewery.** First licensed 1853. The old de-licensed country inn was offered for sale by auction at the Darsham Hall, Chesham in 1958 and is now a private house. See the original sign pictured on the inside back cover.

ST LEONARDS

No.38 The White Lion

Dates from: **1714.** Known brewery suppliers: **Weller's** (to 1930) / **Benskin's / Allied Breweries / Punch.** Samuel Baldwin was the first licensee. The Bishop family were tenants for over 100 years until 1954. The White Lion remains a traditional, characterful country pub offering real ales and good food.

STILL SERVING

SWAN BOTTOM

No.39 *The Red Lion*

Dates from: **late 18th century**. Closed as a public house in May 1938 when an application to transfer its licence to the Boot & Slipper in Amersham was refused. Now a private residence.

No.40 *The Old Swan*

Location: **Kingswood.** Dates from: **1542.** An old coaching inn, now much extended and a thriving country pub. Large flower and vegetable gardens with seating. Low beamed, traditional interior with a restaurant in the side extension.

THE LEE

No.41 *The Cock and Rabbit*

Dates from: **1646**. Also known as: **The Cock and Coney**. Was moved brick by brick across The Green in 1908 when the Liberty family owned most of the village, and chose to move the pub further from the Manor House (the old pub is pictured and the rebuilt structure is illustrated). It originally had stables at the rear, but was considerably extended in 1932 and 1985. The Liberty family sold the pub in 1970 and it is now under Italian management, with resulting fine food (including the Graziemille restaurant) and a good reputation which brings in visitors from far afield.

WHELPLEY HILL

No.42 *The White Hart*

The original building was a farmer's cottage dating back to the **15th century**. First licensed in 1830 – the artist's impression is of the building before extension. The pub has had just three landlords in the last 100 years. It was a favourite watering hole for the US Air Force personnel stationed at Bovingdon during WWII. The officers' mess was a lean-to shed in the back garden.

US servicemen would also visit The Three Horseshoes (pictured) at Pudds Cross, just over the Hertfordshire border. The last landlady of this pub, which closed in the 1960s, was Dolly Bragg, an accomplished pianist and quite a character!

The White Hart still has evidence of a tunnel running from the cellar to Barton Colliers, possibly a priest run. Regulars of The White Hart were featured in Tony Harman's television series *Seventy Summers*, the story of a Chiltern farm.

Today, this tucked-away pub serves the small community of Whelpley Hill and the surrounding villages on the Hertfordshire border. It serves good food and has a wonderful family garden.

STILL SERVING

REFERENCES

Baines, A. and Birch, C., *A Chesham Century*, 1994

Birch, C. and Armistead, J., *Yesterday's Town: Chesham*, 1977

Hay, D. & J., *Hilltop Villages of the Chilterns*, 1983

Hunt, J., *Chesham – A Pictorial History*, 1997

Piggin, G., *Tales of Old Chesham*, 1993

Piggin, G., *More Tales of Old Chesham*, 1995

Seabright, C., *Chesham in Old Picture Postcards*, vols. 1-3, 1985-1995

Seabright, C., *Chesham Yesterday & Today*, 1996

Seabright, C., *Images of England – Chesham*, 2004

Chesham & District Directory, 1914-1915

Chesham Bois – A Celebration of the Village and its History, 1999

Chesham Museum website: www. cheshammuseum.org.uk

Chesham Tapestry booklet, 1974

Chesham Town Talk magazine, 1994-2006

Kelly's Directory of Chesham & Amersham, 1847-1941

Resources at the Centre For Buckinghamshire Studies, Aylesbury

Resources at the Chesham Study Centre, Chesham Library

Tithe map and assessment, 1842

ACKNOWLEDGEMENTS

The majority of the old images in this book were collected by **Ray East**, and the photographers remain anonymous. The 19th century photographers, such as **William Butts** and **William Coles**, often signed their images or printed their details alongside. Ray East also took some of the photos from the 1980s and '90s himself. All the recent photographs were taken by the authors and also by **Ian Freeman**. The detailed line arts (unless otherwise stated) are printed with the kind permission of **Ron Quirk**. The wonderful artist's impressions are the work of **Madeleine Fletcher**. Three watercolours are reproduced thanks to **Barry Holt**. A few of the old photos were lent to us by the author and local historian **Colin Seabright,** and we are grateful for his help. The view of Chesham Brewery on p6 and the details of the watercolour by Thomas Fisher on pp10 & 17 are © **Buckinghamshire County Museum.** The Brewery sign is courtesy of **Jo Franks.** The line drawing of The Angel is taken from the Chesham Tapestry booklet. We are grateful to **Richard Saunders** for access to the collection of Arnold Long's images, mostly of Ley Hill. Thank you to **Carolyn & Philip Thomas** and **Malcolm Rixon** at Broadway Baptist Church for access to their archives. Also to **Sue Gordon** for access to the collection of images held by Chesham Museum, and **Shay Comaskey, Steve & Pat Miller** for the photo of The Griffin. The sketch of The Pheasant, Waterside is by **Mr H Fletcher** and the painting of the horse entering The Stag is by **George Bridges.** The line drawing of The Star & Garter, now an antiques shop, is courtesy of **Miss Hearn** and **Elaine Bamford.** The line drawing of The Three Tuns is by **Harry Bates.** The photo of the family outside The Waggon & Horses and also of William Moore's, Townsend Road is by kind permission of **Bill and Hazel Moore.** The photo of the Botley Rover is courtesy of **Rita Richardson** and those of The Bricklayers Arms are courtesy of **Wendy Smith**. The line drawing of The Rose & Crown, Hawridge is courtesy of **Sandra Taylor**. Thank you to **Roy Morton** and the landlord of The Plough for information and photos on Hyde Heath. The line drawing of The Old Swan is thanks to the landlady of that establishment. The Maurice Stratford painting is courtesy of **Gwen Simmonds.** The Lamb at Potter Cross sign and photo thanks to **Mr & Mrs L A Payne.** The photo of the Black Horse, South Heath thanks to **Caroline Owen-Thomas**. We are particularly indebted to the **Cholesbury cum St Leonards Local History Group** for providing old photographs of The White Lion, St Leonards; The Boot & Slipper, Buckland Common; The Full Moon, Hawridge; The Plough, Chivery; The Rose & Crown, Hawridge and The Rose & Crown, Buckland Common. See p4 for details of the cover illustrations. Thanks also to: **Peter Antonio, Shirley Blomfield, Peter Broom, Chris Brown, Pete Bruton, Bill Gardiner, Sheila Hart, Bryan How, Bill Ivory, Carol Popple, Neil Rees, John & Angela Skrimshire, Don Taylor, Joyce Taylor, David Tuffney, Jenny Walker, Joan & Margaret Walton** and **Jenny Willment**. Keith Fletcher and Peter Hawkes made it their mission to visit all of those pubs which are still serving and wish to thank the proprietors for their help with the research.

THE AUTHORS

Ray East was born in Chesham in 1927. He spent most of his working life as a skilled garage mechanic and MOT tester. On retirement, Ray decided to record his home town in photographs. As a founder member of Chesham Camera Club, he pursued a keen interest in black-and-white photography, processing and printing. He also spent many years collecting and archiving old photographs which he copied from his many contacts in Chesham. Ray was often seen about town with bicycle and camera until recent failing eyesight has limited his hobby. To witness much of his collection published is a longterm ambition fulfilled. Photo: Anne Crabbe

Keith Fletcher was born in Chesham in 1940. He has lived in the town all his life except for two years in the United States. A qualified physicist by training, he spent most of his working life with Amersham International, formerly The Radiochemical Centre. Since taking early retirement, Keith has developed his interest in local history and now writes and lectures on the topic. He has produced monographs on the local Co-operative Society and on brickmaking in the area, and writes an on-going series of articles on Chesham personalities and achievers in *Chesham Town Talk* magazine. Keith also runs the Chesham Fingerstyle Guitar Club. His wife Madeleine has provided several sketches for this book. Photo: Ian Freeman

Peter Hawkes was born in Chesham in 1966 and grew up in Ley Hill village. He has run a graphic design and publishing business since 1990. A keen local historian, he is a founder member of Chesham Museum – The Stables. The Hawkes family has lived in the town since historical records began, and Peter's great-great-grandfather was landlord of The Prince's Arms. His forebears also ran The Bell, The Tap, The Blue Ball and The Queen's Head at various times. Peter hopes that this will be the first in a series of books based on the Ray East Collection. Photo: Anne Crabbe

INDEX

including pub names and surnames (street names generally not included)